• • •

Social (Media) by Design

...

Social (Media) by Design

*A social media how-to guide that teaches the
simple steps to a successful social presence*

**Paige Gibson & Tatum Major & Johannah Saari
& Emily Sullivan & Kaylee Weycker**

• • •

PROLOGUE

Today's world is constantly evolving. What was trending yesterday probably isn't trending today. So in a world of constant changes of terms, platforms, audiences, brands, etc. how do you keep up with social media? Are you looking to develop a cutting-edge social media strategy that will set you apart from your competition? Without a proper strategy it can be overwhelming.

Let this book be your social media how-to guide. The collaboration of five social media experts resulted in Social (Media) by Design. Whether you are looking to take the first steps in your social media journey or are looking to improve your preexisting social media presence—let our tips guide you.

This book explains the process from the beginning. Those who are just starting can establish a solid foundation, amateurs can make sure they are headed the right direction and fellow experts can continue their social media education. It is a win-win for everyone. We hope you enjoy.

● ● ●

ACKNOWLEDGEMENTS

There are many people who influenced our book and helped us along the way. We would like to acknowledge all of our family, friends, and roommates who read our book numerous times, when asked, "Does this sound ok?!" We appreciate your patience and ongoing support.

In particular, we would like to give a tremendous thank you to Bruce Moorehouse for encouraging this book and supporting us the entire way, as well as Michelle Fitzgerald for inspiring and influencing the book.

One last acknowledgement goes to a former Professor Davis for helping to edit our book, thank you dearly for your time.

TABLE OF CONTENTS

· · ·

INTRODUCTION- SOCIAL (MEDIA) BY DESIGN

So, for one reason or another, you have decided to devote your time to improving your presence on social media. Throughout this book we will be explaining key terms, ideas and concepts that will help you do just that. "Social media" has become a very large, overarching umbrella term. In this book, we will be referring to social media as "the collective of online communication channels dedicated to community based input, interaction, content sharing and collaboration."[1]

To begin, it is important for you to understand why social media has become such an influence on our society today. Conversation is innate to human behavior. Due to humans' altruistic attitude, we naturally look to help and bond with others.[2] People have a longing to connect and receive feedback. Social media mirrors what humans have been doing throughout their whole existence—creating communities to converse, and learn from one another. Technology has provided us a way to share our story beyond just a verbal communication

---

1 Fitzgerald, M. September 8th 2015. Social Media. Lecture presented at Social Media AD and PR in University of St. Thomas, Saint Paul.
2 Nice Guys Finish First, David Brooks, May 16th 2001, NY Times – Sept. 30th 2015

and to a much broader audience than just those we live by. **Humans are social by design.** Social design is a concept that plays off the need to share and connect with others.

What is social design? A simple explanation of Social design is "a product or strategy that encourages and facilitates conversation."[3] So, conversation, understood in this sense, is the means by which we communicate who we are to others while receiving feedback and acquiring information from those same people. Socially-designed products or strategies put people at the center of the experience. This is a newer shift in the way in which the Internet has been used and structured. This newer approach actually is a closer reflection to how society has always functioned.

---

3 Fitzgerald, M. October 6th 2015. Social Media. Lecture presented at Social Media AD and PR in University of St. Thomas, Saint Paul.

We have found there is a lack of information regarding the basic and simple steps to create a successful social media strategy. Throughout this book, we intend to inform and teach you the fundamentals of social media through the concept of social design. We have created our own visual, that we named the Strategic SM Matrix, to show how each step is necessary for the whole structure to stand solid. Each chapter will guide you on the importance of each topic and how to implement each concept into your own social design.

RESEARCH

To begin, you are going to want to spend time researching. This portion is going to include familiarizing yourself with the various social media platforms, so you can choose the best ones to connect with your audience. Knowing your way around all the outlets will give you a distinct advantage: having a versatile campaign. This initial research will be the foundation to your social presence.

BRAND

You need to know who you are and how to present that on social media. There are various ways to do this, and we cover them throughout this chapter. This section is important for developing your brand. It will help you figure out what your brand is, who it is for, what values it holds, and how you can accurately represent those ideals.

STRATEGIZE

This step is the most time consuming, but is arguably the most important. A myth about social media is that it sort of "just happens," that companies just post whatever they want. This couldn't be further from the truth. A successful social media campaign is well thought-out, analyzed, and scrutinized over a number of times. Part of your strategy will be setting social media objectives, selecting a target audience, and preparing content tailored to said audience. This step requires creativity and may be frustrating at times, but, if done well, will yield a fantastic product in the form of a successful campaign.

IMPLEMENT

Once the organization of your content is complete, you must share it with the social world. As your campaign runs its course, there will be various ways to compliment it. Hashtagging is an excellent way to accentuate your brand as different topics become relevant to your target audience. Another way for your campaign to gain traction is to partner with bloggers. Both will help your campaign gain popularity and we cover them in this stage.

MEASURE

The final piece of the puzzle, and the last chapter of this book, is to measure your results. The only way to know how successful your campaign has been is to measure your results in relation to your objectives and goals. In this section, we suggest various ways to analyze your data that you've collected. This analysis will give you better insights on your social campaign.

We took our experiences, our research, and our knowledge and combined them all into this social media brand bible. We hope that you can take the whole book, or even just bits and pieces, and use it to help your social presence. Social media is not going to go away, and if you want your brand to stay relevant, you not only need to join the social media world, you need to have a strong and effective social campaign.

SECTION I Research

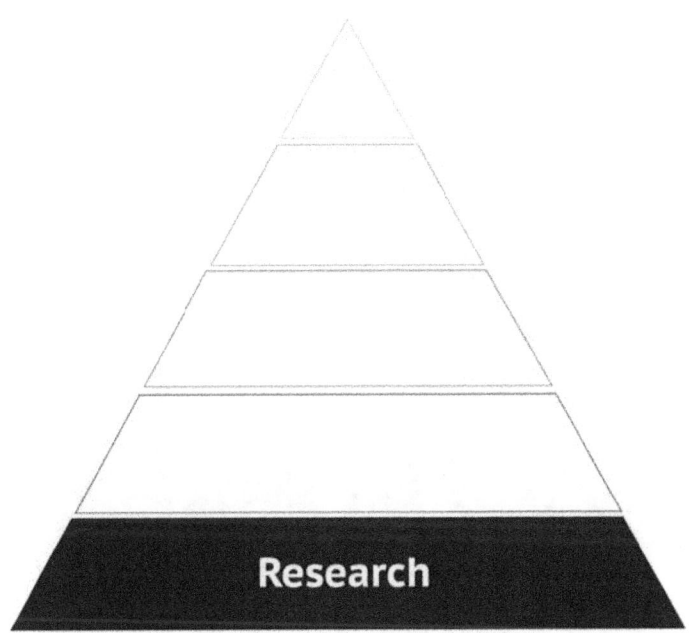

• • •

SOCIAL MEDIA: A QUICK OVERVIEW TO FINDING YOUR FIT

There are plenty of ways to promote your business, your company, and yourself. For example, businesses have used word of mouth, billboards, newspaper advertisements, and brochures to promote themselves. Those options were the main focus of the past, but no longer are those the only options available. Since you live in the "now", you need to become familiar with the technology and social media that exist. There are many different platforms you can use to promote yourself. However, these platforms are constantly changing. One platform we use now could easily become obsolete to the next big thing. For now, we will focus on what is most used by the majority of social media consumers in 2015. The following chapter will help build the foundation of our Strategic Matrix— Research.

STYLES AND PLATFORMS

Social media is all around us. It's unavoidable. However, this is not a bad thing. As a smart and effective social media campaigner, there are multiple ways to put yourself out there and join in on the buzz. Here's a quick overview of the different styles and platforms of current and popular social media:

- **Social Networks** allow one to connect with others—personally or professionally. "A social network site is a social media site that allows users to connect and share with people who have similar interests and backgrounds." [4] Today, most social networks are now mobile-first, meaning that users of each social site are accessing and posting from their smartphones.

    Facebook and LinkedIn are examples of social network sites. Facebook has 1.49 billion monthly active users, and 44% of those users only log in on a mobile device. [5] Currently, LinkedIn has 364 million members. [6]

- **Micro-blogs** are sites that allow short form content. They are primarily time sensitive and are used to post short and quick messages or advertisements.
    - o Twitter is the best example for a micro-blog. Twitter allows its users to only post 140 characters per tweet. There are 288 million users on Twitter a month. The service sees more than 500 million tweets per day. 80%

---

4 The 6 Types of Social Media. (n.d.). Retrieved October 22, 2015, from http://seo-pressor.com/social-media-marketing/types-of-social-media/
5 Facebook: Monthly active users 2015 | Statistic. (n.d.). Retrieved October 22, 2015, from http://www.statista.com/statistics/264810/number-of-monthly-active-facebook-users-worldwide/
6 LinkedIn: Numbers of members 2015 | Statistic. (n.d.). Retrieved October 22, 2015, from http://www.statista.com/statistics/274050/quarterly-numbers-of-linkedin-members/

of Twitter's active monthly users access the service on a mobile device.[7]

- **Blogs** are sites that allow long form content. They allow the blogger to control the discussion. Think of a blog as an online journal with other users being able to respond to your entries and posts.
  - o Tumblr, Blogger, and Wordpress are all great examples of blogs.
- **Media Sharing** websites allow users to share different types of media, such as photos and videos. These sites enable sharing across different platforms.
  - o YouTube, Instagram, and Vine are all media sharing sites. Users watch 6 billion hours of video on YouTube every month. [8] There are over 300 million monthly users on Instagram [9] and the users choose to share photos and fifteen-second videos of whatever they want the world to see. Vine is a site that only allows its users to upload six-second videos. There are 200 million monthly active users on Vine. [10]

Now that you have a basic understanding of the different types of social media, it is time to decide which ones are the best for you and your company.

7 Langer, E. (2015, March 20). 140 things you don't know about Twitter. Retrieved October 22, 2015, from http://www.cnbc.com/2014/03/21/140-things-you-dont-know-about-twitter.html

8 Marshall, C. (2014, September 3). 33 Amazing YouTube Facts and Stats to Tweet and Share. Retrieved October 22, 2015, from http://www.reelseo.com/youtube-facts-stats-2014/

9 Instagram monthly active users 2015 | Statistic. (n.d.). Retrieved October 22, 2015, from http://www.statista.com/statistics/253577/number-of-monthly-active-instagram-users/

10 Smith, C. (2014, August 24). 25 Amazing Vine Statistics. Retrieved October 22, 2015, from http://expandedramblings.com/index.php/vine-statistics/

THE BEST FIT FOR YOU

How do I know which social media platforms I should use? Which platforms are the best fit for me? What are the benefits of each? How can I be sure my message will reach my base?

These are probably the big questions you have going through your head right now. Don't panic. We are here to help you answer these questions.

First, familiarize yourself with the platforms—log on to the sites, check them out, do some research and see what you like. Which of these is going to be most beneficial to you? Maybe it's media sharing and you want to put yourself, your company, your product, etc. out there and share videos and photos to give followers a glimpse of your product. Maybe you want to connect personally with others, so you turn to Facebook and post there in order to connect with your friends and followers by posting relevant information and responding to questions and comments. Whichever platforms you choose, keep in mind the goals of your company and who your audience is—which we will touch on in a later chapter in this book.

Keep in mind that the decision of which platform(s) to use need to factor in a number of variables, such as the number of users you wish to reach, the content you wish to post, and the demographics of the consumers you wish to appeal to. The more users a social site has, the more reach you will have. you can promote your brand to a bigger audience more effectively. For example, Twitter has 288 million users on its site per month, so if you went with this platform, your company has the potential to reach out to, or be noticed by a large number of users. As far as the content you choose to post, you need to look at the different social media available to you and determine which site will be best for you. If your company is selling baked goods in a small market stand type of setting, you probably won't want to post to LinkedIn, because that platform is aimed at business professionals. You would want people to see your products, so posting photos on Instagram or journaling and sharing recipes on Tumblr would be a much more effective way to start out. When it comes to demographics, one big concept you should think about is the age of your target market. Find out which platforms have the most users in the age group you want to reach out to, and start promoting yourself on that platform.

As stated before, social media is unavoidable. It is constantly changing and a great way to promote yourself and your company. The way things used to be is no longer relevant. It is time to live in the present and do your research to find your niche. The base of our Strategic Matrix encourages and helps you to get out there and find which platforms best suit you.

FAST REFERENCE GUIDE:

- ✓ Become familiar with styles and platforms
- ✓ Research demographics of audience you want to reach out to
- ✓ Research platforms and decide which ones are the best fit

SECTION II Brand

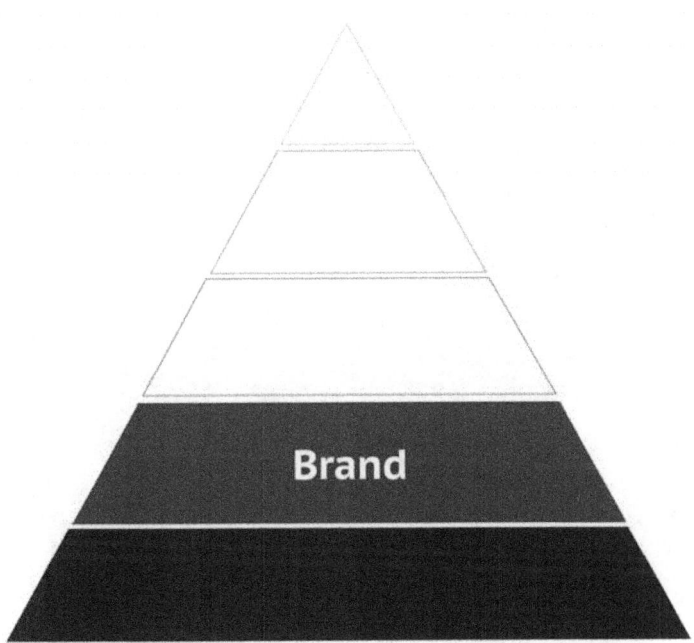

• • •

SOCIAL MEDIA BRANDING BASICS

Where do I begin with branding? In order to successfully begin branding your social media it's crucial to understand what branding is. In his book, "Your Brand the Next Media Company," Michael Brito explains branding as:

> "A product, service, or concept that is publicly distinguished from other products, services, or concepts so that it can be easily communicated and usually marketed. A brand name is the name of the distinctive product, service, or concept. Branding can be applied to the entire corporate identity as well as to individual product and service names." [11]

Wait, what does that even mean? In simpler terms, Brito is saying that potential or repeat customers think of your business name with a

---

11 Brito, M. (2014). Defining your Brand Story and Content Narrative. In *Your brand, the Next Media Company.* Que Publishing

product, service, or concept. Whether you're a startup or an established corporation, it has now become essential for your brand to have a presence on social media. For example, there are roughly 161 million daily average users in the United States and Canada on Facebook, and two thirds of people registered on Facebook use it daily. [12] That's a huge number of people that could potentially be reached, and Facebook is just one social platform!

One thing that any company or organization has to its benefit is that beginning to use social media is free. However, the challenge that comes with using something free is that anyone with access to the Internet can as well. "Brand marketers are no longer just buying audience. They are the ones who are participating in the conversation by creating and distributing content to their audience directly." [13] People will filter out whatever they believe to be irrelevant, which means you'll need to take the steps to stand out in relation to your competition. You want your consumers participating in the brand conversation, not ignoring your content.

BRANDING ESSENTIALS: WHAT YOU NEED TO IDENTIFY

Now that you know what branding your business means, let's get started. "For you to reach them with your brand message, you need to manufacture an environment where you are creating, curating, and aggregating relevant content at the right time, in the right channel, and to the right customer." [14] Brito begins to explain in more detail

---

12 Fitzgerald, M. September 8th 2015. Social Media. Lecture presented at Social Media AD and PR in University of St. Thomas, Saint Paul.

13 Brito, M. (2014). Defining your Brand Story and Content Narrative. In *Your brand, the Next Media Company.* Que Publishing

14 Brito, M. (2014).

what everyone looking to brand their business, service, or concept must know before moving forward. [15] Summarized below are the five points that are essential to understand when beginning to brand:

- **Brand Position**
  - o This describes what your company does, what your unique value is, and how a customer would benefit from using your product or service. You want to make sure that with each post you create you remember the brand position. It should be clear to potential consumers what your brand or service you are offering. For example, Wal-Mart's brand position is focused on delivering a low cost product to the consumer.
- **Brand Promise**
  - o The center of any marketing plan should be the promise your brand is making to its customers. Think about it this way: *Why should customers choose us? What makes us unique? What makes us the best choice?* These questions should guide your every interaction with the consumer. For example, TOMS shoes donates one pair of shoes to a child in a third world country for each pair sold. When they promote their brand, that is the center of their marketing campaigns. Consumers know that if they are looking for a new pair of shoes, they can make a purchase of TOMS and help contribute to the greater good which helps ease the guilt of spending. For some, the added aspect of philanthropy with their purchase is enough of a reason to choose TOMS over a competing brand.

---

15 Brito, M. (2014).

- **Brand Personality**
  - This is what your company wants its brand to be known for. As a person, there are specific personality traits that you possess and people will associate with you. *Are you optimistic? Pessimistic? Are you a leader or a follower?* Think of your business in the same way. What traits would you want customers to associate with your brand? For example, head over to theindiechicks.com. Looking at their webpage, it's incredibly easy to identify what their brand position is. Add the website to your bookmarks tab. What should appear is their logo, followed by the statement "the voice of self-empowered women". Even if you decide that you never want to visit theindiechicks. com webpage ever again, you'll know exactly who they are and what kind of website it is without even clicking on it.
- **Brand Story**
  - Your company or organization's history. It's important for customers to understand where you are coming from. It adds credibility, shows how you have experienced growth, provides a summary of your products or services, and really highlights aspects of what makes your brand special. A great example of this is when Google introduced Chrome. A video showed a father journaling his daughter's milestones. The video was used numerous Google products and services to show how you, the consumer, can use Google's suite of products for so much more than just sending an email or searching a term.
- **Brand Association**
  - Physical attributes that would initiate people thinking of your brand. This would be your name, logo, colors,

taglines, fonts, images, or even a sound.[16] Lets go back to theindiechicks.com webpage for this example. Their logo, tab, bookmark, and design are all incredibly cohesive. Across all of those channels, the reader will know that pink, black, and a certain heading font will be present. Now, when they see that color scheme or font, especially combined, they'll associate it with your brand.

BRANDING INSPIRATION: NETFLIX

If you're having a difficult time identifying strong ideas of what you want your brand to be known for, start considering what you do *not* want your brand to be known for. Netflix released their long-term review report where they identified what their role will be as streaming television shows and movies on the Internet begins to replace traditional television usage. Although it addressed the things that Netflix wants to be known for, it also went into detail of what they do *not* want to be known for. They focus on streaming, saying that they want that to be associated with their brand and not a "Do everything brand: Starbucks, nor 7-Eleven; Southwest, not United; HBO, not Dish. We are about flat-free unlimited viewing commercial-free."[17] They don't stop there, however. Going into even more detail, they further define their brand as "a movie and TV series entertainment network." Although they begin with a larger statement, they progressively add detail to further define what their brand stands for and wants to be known for. Giving contrasts based on strengths of one company compared to another is also facilitating the conversation for

---

16 Brito, M. (2014). Defining your Brand Story and Content Narrative. In *Your brand, the Next Media Company.* Que Publishing

17 Netflix View: Internet TV is replacing Linear TV

customers to recognize what sets Netflix apart from any other online streaming service.

Understanding how you want consumers to see your brand is a great place to start. Even if it is a simple statement, it can be expanded upon as you work on your social media branding and strategy. Create a company brand with a story that will compel customers to not only use your brand, but endorse your brand as well.

BRAND CONVERSATION: PHILANTHROPY AND STORYTELLING

"Features tell, benefits sell." Your company does not have to be rooted in philanthropy, but it's important to consider conveying the message that your company does care about the greater good. When curating social media content that actively depicts your brand, you should be telling a story, and the majority of people love a story with a happy ending. Showing new and old customers that you care about the bigger picture by being aware of the conversations and community perceptions of your brand is incredibly important. *Are they validating your narrative? Do they refer to your brand in a way you want them to?* If you answer "no" to either question, start from step one and see where you can improve.

• • •

PUBLIC RELATIONS IN SOCIAL MEDIA

Public relations is the practice of managing communication between a particular organization and its publics. Any organization has a number of potential publics. Whether it be using technology like social media to gain exposure or sharing information to a third party source, public relations is about creating both positive and strong publicity. Public relations is a key aspect in any business structure. This could be communicating with prospective clients, consumers and brands or reaching out to media outlets. The social media development has only helped in the business realm of public relations. Social media is now a major resource to use for sharing and creating content that aids in social interaction and brand engagement.

Everyone can think of a brand that they both like and dislike. Now that social media has engulfed our social interaction, it gives the consumers a platform to voice their opinions outwardly. Because of the relaxed nature and easiness of social media, it now makes conversation happen rapidly. Presently, the everyday person is now a marketer through social media. If you Instagram a picture of your dog next to a Starbucks cup, you are indirectly advertising free of charge for Starbucks. Everything you do on social media now has the ability to make a large number of people notice, sometimes so much so that the action has the potential to become what we call viral. With that, there is now more brand engagement than ever before because of social media. Conversations are constantly being had about brands that can help a brand greatly or tear it to shreds in the eyes of the public.

Social media now influences a mass audience to send and receive messages, especially in public relations. Tweets, comments, likes, and followers all contribute to the effectiveness of your digital message. Now, consumers can gain distribution of brands and businesses through social channels just as brands can learn more than ever about their consumers.

Using social channels in your public relations plan, such as an Internet blogger, can help target even a wider audience with other followers for a larger distribution channel. Social media completely impacts all digital media and other major media channels today, which attributes to practicing how to use each channel correctly with your PR message and direction.

Consumers more so now than ever before are completely engaged with social media and companies are seeing the power and affect that their brand can have with a great social media reputation. Brands are now using these tools to increase their own popularity whilst growing brand followers in the process. Social media branding strategy is the plan of using social media in a deliberate way to advertise and obtain interest in a brand, company or overall campaign. By using new and unique strategies, a brand can flourish within social media and directly to consumers. Companies need social brand strategy especially in regards to public relations. Having a strong strategy and tactic behind your social media engagement and posts is critical in developing a prosperous public relations strategy. For example, tweeting main facts from a social campaign will highlight the client without making the reader read a long press release. Social media creates short snippets of quick information, something that the public is drawn to. A story can be the most viral and acknowledge when told through the right social channel. Instagram images, Youtube videos, GIF's and vines have become some of the most popular outlets to share information as people are drawn to quick yet creative content. Social media allows the fluff of usual content to be deleted so that your social platforms will be tailored to specific content that matters.

Now PR professionals can blog their campaigns, tweet using hashtag strategies to engage in a conversation, or run a 6-second video about the importance of their media message. Now, the options within these social platforms have become endless. The consumer power that social media allows engages the public be an incredible influence. This is where brands and businesses need to be extremely precautious when engaging with social media users owned content.

An example of how this could go wrong without taking the right precautions comes from a New York Times Article titled "On Instagram and Other Social Media, Redefining User Engagement".[18] This article further explains how Shereen Way posted a picture on her personal Instagram account of her 4-year old daughter wearing a pair of cute, pink Crocs. Shereen Way posted this photo with the hashtag #Crocs which later was pulled from a pool of similar hashtags and put onto the Crocs website showcasing her 4-year old daughter. Ms. Way claims that Crocs had not reached out to pull her personal photo to their stockpile and she felt it was odd. This is an example of where to draw the line with consumer engagement and user-generated content.

---

18 Ember, S., & Abrams, R. (2015, September 20). On Instagram and Other Social Media, Redefining 'User Engagement'. Retrieved November 8, 2015.

Crocs then released a statement saying, "It believed it was acting consistently with social media marketing best practices." "We are continually evaluating our practices and welcome consumer feedback," the company said. "It's our policy to get permission before making any other use of photos consumers have tagged us in."[19] Although user generated content is definitely a communicative and interactive way to connect with consumers, it also needs to be taken into precaution with the user's complete consent to earn both brand loyalty and trust.

FAST REFERENCE GUIDE:

- ✓ Identify your brand
- ✓ Create brand conversation
- ✓ Social media and its optimization of public relations platforms
- ✓ The everyday person is now becoming a marketer through social media
- ✓ Social media allowing mass target audiences to send and receive messages
- ✓ Social media strategies and tactics
- ✓ How to safely use user generated content with your brand and business

19 Ember, S., & Abrams, R. (2015, September 20). On Instagram and Other Social Media, Redefining 'User Engagement'. Retrieved September 8, 2015 http://www.nytimes.com/2015/09/21/business/media/retailers-use-of-their-fans-photos-draws-scrutiny.html?_r=0.

SECTION III Strategize

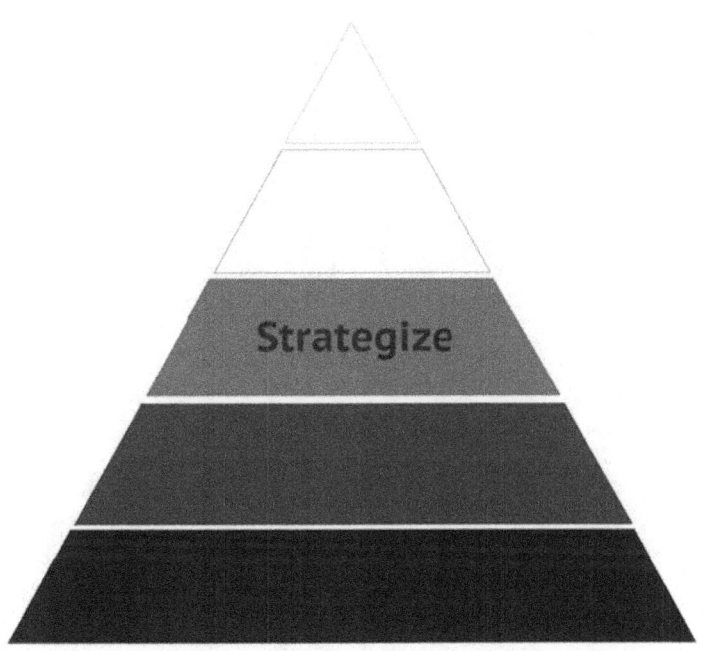

• • •

FINDING YOUR AUDIENCE

When using social media to brand yourself, it is important to not only know and establish who you are as a person or company, but to know whom you are reaching out to and targeting as your audience. While it's crucial to know what you want to post to get your brand across to your customers, it's important to realize which social media sites reach out to the audience you want to influence the most. In this chapter, we will help you understand how to find your target audience, which fits into the "Strategize" step in our Strategic Matrix.

KNOW YOUR AUDIENCE

Not everyone uses every type of social media—like Twitter, Instagram, and Facebook—and that's perfectly fine. When branding yourself as a company, it is important that you are posting the appropriate content on the appropriate social media site or app. For example, your YouTube channel should be filled with videos that keep your audience's attention. To do this, make the videos short and interesting enough to leave your audience wanting more. Maybe your audience is not a video streaming market. Perhaps they want a quick and easy read on Facebook or Twitter. Most millennials tend not to be able to even sit through a thirty-second advertisement on YouTube without hitting the "skip" button.

In today's world, it is all about the apps and emojis. Domino's is a company that seems to have its audience figured out. The company has realized that their consumers want the ease of conveniently ordering a pizza online by simply sending Domino's Twitter handle a pizza emoji. As if ordering pizza was not already at your fingertips, Domino's may have changed the delivery game forever. "It's the epitome of convenience," Patrick Doyle, Domino's CEO, told USA Today. "We've got this down to a five-second exchange." [20] Domino's is a great example of a company knowing its audience and taking advantage of social media in order to change how customers can order food.

Another company we can take a look at is Budweiser. This beer company knows exactly who their audience is and how to reach out to it. They know what their audience likes, given the fact that Budweiser has been using Clydesdales in their commercials since 1987. They've since launched a YouTube channel and various hashtag campaigns such as #GrabSomeBuds, #MadeInAmerica, and #ThisBudsForYou on Twitter. The tweets have exploded and have created quite the buzz. Budweiser has also been reaching out to an even younger audience between the ages of twenty-one and twenty-seven because they have found that 44% of this drinking age group has never tried Budweiser. [21] Since they knew exactly who they wanted to reach out

20 Mosbergen, D. (2015, May 13). You'll Soon Be Able To Order Domino's Pizza On Twitter, Via Pizza Emoji. Retrieved October 22, 2015, from http://www.huffington-post.com/2015/05/13/dominos-pizza-emoji-twitter_n_7272138.html

21 Boyer, L. (2014, November 24). Budweiser Ditches Clydesdales to Focus Advertising on Younger Audience. Retrieved October 22, 2015, from http://www.usnews.com/news/articles/2014/11/24/budweiser-ditches-clydesdales-to-focus-advertising-on-younger-audience

to as their target audience, they switched up their social media, specifically their YouTube channel, and made commercials asking millenials the simple question of: "If you could grab a Bud with any of your friends these holidays, who would it be?" They also took to their Twitter page to ask the same question and to launch a holiday Budweiser campaign with the hashtag #HolidayBuds. Knowing who your audience is makes a huge difference for your social media branding.

ATTRACTION

Once you have figured out who your audience is, the next step is to decide what it is about your brand or company that is going to attract consumers to you. Perhaps it is your hashtag all over Twitter, Instagram and Facebook. If it's clever and creative enough, your target audience will become attracted to it and follow the hashtag closely on their social media. The goal itself is to get your target audience to use your hashtag appropriately where they see fit. The more attractive your social media outlets are, the more your audience grows. Thus meaning, the more your audience grows, the stronger your name recognition becomes in your market.

Think about what else is going to attract consumers to you. Is it a horribly put-together, black-and-white Tumblr or Facebook page? No! It is an organized, thought-out, vibrant, hip, fun, exciting, and colorful page. Your target audience is not going to click through your profiles if they are mundane and not updated often. It's important that you post to your social media frequently and are able to keep it updated. It's also attractive to consumers if you interact with them on your social media. For example, one day, one of the authors tweeted to Gatorade telling them how amazing one of their flavors was, and they tweeted her back! Being the excited woman that she is, she freaked out over a simple "Thank you" tweet back. She was pretty pumped up that Gatorade had noticed her, so she sent a follow up tweet exclaiming how awesome it was that Gatorade had a small interaction with her. It goes to show, that being engaged on your social media platforms is an attractive quality to possess and a must-have when you want to brand yourself and connect with your audience.

GOALS

After finding your audience and figuring out what is going to attract it to your social media, you need to figure out what your purpose is and what goals you want to accomplish. SMART Goals, is a tool you can use when setting goals for yourself and your company. "A SMART goal is defined as one that is specific, measurable, achievable, results-focused, and time-bound." [22]

S- Specific. Define the goal. Who is involved? What do you want to accomplish? Where will it be done? Why are you doing this?

M- Measurable. How are you going to track the progress and measure the outcome?

A- Attainable. Is the goal reasonable enough to be accomplished?

R- Realistic. Is the goal worthwhile? Will it meet your needs? Is it reasonable?

T- Timely. This is the time limit of your goal.

---

22 Writing S.M.A.R.T. Goals. (n.d.). Retrieved October 22, 2015, from http://www.hr.virginia.edu/uploads/documents/media/Writing_SMART_Goals.pdf

Section III Strategize

Now that you have a feel for SMART Goals, you can think about what you really want to get out of your social media outlets. Maybe you set a goal of gaining 100 thousand followers on your social media or want to interact with a certain number of consumers per day. Whatever your goals are, make sure they are attainable, and that you and your social media team are up for the challenge of accomplishing them.

• • •

SETTING SOCIAL MEDIA OBJECTIVES AND STRATEGIES

A strong social media business strategy will define how a company or brand uses social media to benefit the corporation. It is a documented plan of action that helps an organization stay aligned internally and externally. Keeping customers engaged with you and your brand means that they understand who you are and what you stand for. Using your brand position, brand personality, brand story are all great places to start when brainstorming what you would like to accomplish. What consumers see on your social media is the message you send them, so make it impactful!

Building social media objectives and strategies begins by defining what you're hoping for as an outcome. Make your objectives specific, realistic, timed, and measurable. For example, you may want to increase the number of likes on your company's Facebook page, or reach a certain number of "shares" on a photo posted, or maybe gain ten new Twitter followers over the next month.

Make sure that within your planning and strategy process you allow a place to celebrate short-term achievements. If your goal was to gain ten new Twitter followers and you already have eight, take the time to acknowledge that. Conquering social media and creating a brand presence isn't done in simply a few posts!

CONSISTENCY IS KEY

When setting social media objectives and strategies consistency is key. If content is fragmented or scattered, customers will either scroll past it or spend time confused about what your message was. For example, if you're a clothing retailer using Instagram as a platform to promote your brand, the style of photography should be similar so that customers will begin to recognize what content is yours. If some photos are taken at dramatic angles in black and white while others are taken as a "mirror selfie" in color, it can be difficult to understand what the point of the photo and the account as a whole is trying to make. You want the consumer to have a full understanding of what the message is so they will be compelled to share, like, or advocate.

TIMING

It's essential to know which social media platforms your audience is active on. If you were a children's toy company, spending money on marketing with Linkedin would be a waste. Once you've identified where they're active, understand when they're active to understand when the time is to maximize content exposure.

Each social platform has a different time where their users will be more engaged. If you're wanting to use more than one social media channel, the story you're telling needs to have a laser focus.[23] Since the

---

23 Brito, M. (2014). Building Your Content Channel Strategy In *Your brand, the Next Media Company*. Que Publishing

story or content presentation may be altered for different channels it's imperative that the focus of the story is clearly understood. The 140 characters you used for Twitter should probably be elaborated on for the images and caption space that Instagram gives you.

COMMUNICATE INTERNALLY

Having a plan is great but worth nothing if it's not understood. Planned content is always better than something random, so make sure your team understands what is expected. Having a plan is the evolution from "let's try this" to "let's make sure this is adding value to our business." Unclear roles can create conflict so clearly identify roles and responsibilities for those that will be involved in creating social media objectives and content.

"Business units can either be coordinated in their efforts or fragmented and decentralized. Without a common program in place, each business unit develops its own programs, resulting in wasted resources and a fragmented experience for the customer." [24]

Distributing your plan and assigning roles internally can greatly deter the possibility of confusing or fragmented content.

Employees are brand journalists and by keeping them involved, engaged, and excited your objectives can absolutely be obtained. They understand the brand or company better than anyone else, and can work towards telling the story in an engaging manner.

---

24 Brito, M. (2014). Establishing a Centralized "Editorial" Social Business Center of Excellence. In *Your brand, the Next Media Company*. Que Publishing

• • •

CONTENT

In order to be successful in creating and discovering content for your brand's social media strategy, you must first know the different existing types. There are:[25]

Blog Articles- one page articles on topics related to your industry.

White papers- papers that educate your marketplace on an industry trends, challenge, etc. white papers should be about products.

Videos- short two-to three-minute videos about your industry, videos will be the future of social media.

Webinars- live online presentations on an industry topic.

---

25 Halligan, B., & Shah, D. (n.d.). Inbound Marketing: Attact, Engage, and Delight Customer Online.

Podcasts- ten-to 20-minute audio programs or an interview with industry experts similar to radio shows.

Webcasts- live video shows viewed online.

Visuals- content such as info graphics and slide decks.

Now that you know of the different types of content, we can talk about how to yield the most use out of your content.

REPURPOSE AND RECYCLE CONTENT

One of the biggest obstacles in developing an active social platform is having the time to find and create relevant and useful content. Fortunately, your time does not have to be devoted entirely to finding new content. The process of repurposing and recycling (r2) content correctly can you save time while attracting new leads.

What does it mean to r2 content? Although the two may seem nearly identical, both have their own definitions.

To repurpose content is to change the "packaging" from its original state to fit another form of media. An example of this would be turning a webinars' content into multiple blog posts or a single eBook.

To recycle content is to repost something with updated aspects to elongate its shelf life. The shelf life of content is the amount of time it stays "alive" on the platform in which it is shared.

In this section we will cover *why* it is important to r2 content and the different *ways* to do so. By repurposing and recycling content you can achieve the following:[26]

---

26 How to Repurpose Your Social Media Content [Live Webinar]. (n.d.). Retrieved from http://blog.hubspot.com/marketing/repurpose-content-webinar

SAVE TIME

As mentioned earlier, the lack of time is the most common reason organizations are not active on social media. Yes, finding good quality content does take some time but it shouldn't take *all* of your time. Your goal is to find evergreen content, which can best be described as content that is considered sustainable and lasting.[27] Evergreen trees stay green no matter the season, think of evergreen content as the same. An example of content is not necessarily evergreen may be a cultural trend such as joining conversation related to a trending hashtag on twitter.

REACH A WIDER AUDIENCE

By posting to multiple social platforms over time, your chance of reaching new audiences is greatly multiplied. Different people use different types of social media to receive their news whether via visual, long or short text. It may be necessary to alter your content depending on the platform. For example, to convert a webinar into multiple blog posts requires chopping out information to shorten the content.

PROVIDE LASTING VALUE

The second "R" (recycling) becomes especially important when aiming to provide lasting value. Good content needs to have two things, timelessness and significance to the audience. Look back at your previous content to decide what you can alter and republish. If the content is truly "timeless," you may not need to alter anything, just republish. The power of a timely publish date is astounding.

---

27 What Is Evergreen Content? Beginner's Guide to Evergreen Content | WordStream. (n.d.). Retrieved from http://www.wordstream.com/blog/ws/2012/10/16/guide-to-evergreen-content-marketing

As mentioned earlier, by republishing updated content its shelf life is extended. Shelf life varies between platforms. For instance, the shelf life of a social network (i.e. Facebook) will be much longer than that of a micro blog (i.e. Twitter). According to Hubspot the shelf life of a tweet is only about 20 minutes whereas Facebook is about 24 hours.[28]

GIVE GREAT CONTENT THE ATTENTION IT DESERVES

Spending time to find your evergreen content is inevitable, so why let that content go to waste? R2 content as a way to offer your audience additional information, thus adding more value. This doesn't always mean adding excessive amounts of information, it may mean linking to another platform or landing page with the intention to keep people clicking in your backyard. Hubspot specialists claim that a second social media post is twice more likely to be seen and/or shared by the general public than the first.

CONTENT PLANNING: WHAT CONTENT BELONGS ON WHICH PLATFORM

The second most common reason a brand is not active on social media is the confusion associated with content/platform appropriation. The use of personal social media seems much easier due to the lack of "planning" it requires. Think about how you share content on your personal platforms; you may share a short opinion on twitter, a great photo on Instagram, or a link to something interesting that you want to share with family on Facebook. Now take a step back

---

28 How to Repurpose Your Social Media Content [Live Webinar]. (n.d.). Retrieved from http://blog.hubspot.com/marketing/repurpose-content-webinar

and look at your sharing process from a business standpoint. Some content will need to be formatted to fit different types of platforms to mirror what your audience is sharing. It wouldn't make sense to post a lengthy article to twitter or a short opinion on Instagram without a great photo, don't let yourself fall into this trap.

Content appropriation boils down to your intended audience, let's go through the different types of platforms and how they are most commonly used. We have previously gone through a social media landscape overview, lets dig into further detail about content.

SOCIAL NETWORK

As we know, Facebook and LinkedIn are the most common forms of Social Networks today. What is unique about these platforms is the wide audience who is participating. The content in which belongs on a social network platform can be presented in a number of manners. Typically there are no limitations of character count that provides a brand a lot of leeway. Both Facebook and LinkedIn act as fabulous spots for redirection to your Twitter or Instagram for further inter-action. Facebook has become a valuable place for paid advertising to boost your posts. Consider setting aside some funding for social media advertising.

MICRO-BLOGS

An example of a well-known micro-blog is Twitter. As I mentioned earlier, the shelf life of content on twitter is very short compared to other social media platforms. With this being said, Twitter is used primarily for blast updates and news. Consider content for any micro-blog that is timely, fresh and creates conversation. For example, a post redirecting readers to a company update on your website would receive a higher interaction rate than something that is last year's news. Always remember that nearly 80 percent of Twitter users are viewing via mobile device—make content that is responsive!

BLOGS

Two blog platforms (or forums) I am going to focus on are Wordpress and Tumblr. Blogging is so important for a brand because it is a SEO booster. For those who don't know, SEO stands for Search engine optimization and is the process of affecting the visibility of a website or a web page in a search engine's unpaid results.[29] Content that is typically demonstrated on blog sites are visual and informative. It is important to link your blog to your website to create a relationship. Consider multiple blog posts that link to each other, increasing a reader's amount of time spent on your content.

Shameless plug: check out our Tumblr at www.tumblr.com/blog/socialmedia-bydesign

MEDIA SHARING (YOUTUBE, INSTAGRAM)

Media sharing platforms come in many types. YouTube and Instagram are two used by brands in many different ways.

Instagram's audience is primarily younger females. It is important to keep this in mind when creating content. Some examples of successful campaigns running on Instagram are special promotions or contests that are visually stimulating.

---

29 Search engine optimization - Wikipedia, the free encyclopedia. (n.d.). Retrieved November 2, 2015, from https://en.wikipedia.org/wiki/Search_engine_optimization

YouTube has made its way to the center of our culture.[30] It has become the largest video sharing in the world. The most prominent feature of YouTube is that it is compatible with any social media platform to date. Something to keep in mind is that YouTube is a hub for user-generated content (USG). An example of this dates back to Justin Bieber's first song, "One Time." Bieber offered a prize for any fan that could make the most creative music video to his single hit. This resulted in millions of entries and the infamous "Bieber Fever."

Media sharing platforms are the future; consider video based content that you can link to in all other platforms.

FAST REFERENCE GUIDE:

- ✓ Know your audience
- ✓ Attract audience/consumers
- ✓ Set goals
- ✓ Creation of social media strategy
- ✓ Consistency is key
- ✓ Communicate internally
- ✓ Repurpose and Recycle content
- ✓ Find evergreen content that will last
- ✓ Content appropriation is key

---

30 Fitzgerald, M. (2015, September 29). *Social Media Platform Overview* [PowerPoint slides].

SECTION IV Implement

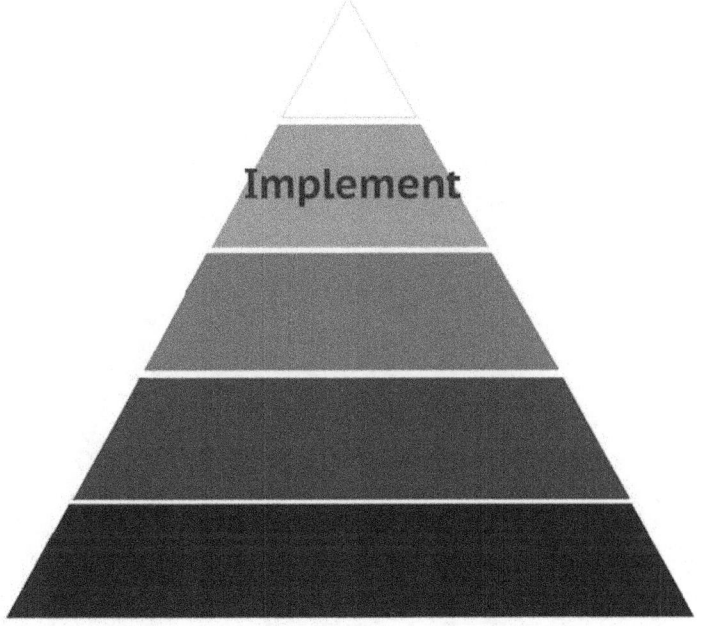

• • •

BLOGGING FOR BRANDS AND BUSINESSES

It has been said to not trust what you read on the Internet, but research shows that now more than ever before, consumers are looking to bloggers before they purchase products. Beauty, lifestyle, fashion, cooking, family-life, travel, cars, light bulbs- there is now a blog for it all. Now, the honesty and transparency that these bloggers write about when talking about their products, experiences and services, perpetuate the consumer into a reasonable source for buying. By connecting with their followers in an open and honest conversation, bloggers are now establishing areas of expertise within the advertising industry and are looked at as a trusted source of information. Currently, the opportunity for a blogger to get their name out there online is just as valuable for a business, as it is for their own personal growth and brand promotion. Companies are now reaching out to well-followed bloggers to help brands seek exposure across more social media platforms.

Every half a second, a new blog is created somewhere in the world.[31] There are hundreds of millions of blogs with endless markets for bloggers to reach their audiences, potentially the fastest form of advertising yet. This type of popular content has developed a growth strategy for brands and businesses to work with as well. Currently, blogging with or for a brand has become the quickest way to earn money for your writing. This is not an ad in a magazine or commercial but likewise, a real person speaking directly about their real experiences and insights. A company that feels their product or brand would be well received by a certain audience are now paying bloggers to advertise for them and promote their products. People are drawn to this type of promotion because it feels personal, and it feels real and truthful. Blogging is a public relations resource in that it uses experts and opinion leaders in the field to give their thoughts on a product. It's a way for the potential consumer to get free publicity about a company or brand. In this case, sometimes the best things in life can definitely be free.

Successful bloggers have indeed built their content to be an immediate source for information or inspiration on a certain topic, especially when their content is uploaded regularly. Your favorite bloggers tend to become sort of like a celebrity to you in which you want to trust their judgment because you genuinely like them. The most success blogs have a trusting and frequented audience that listen to their words of wisdom and trust their judgment. The more trustworthy the blogger, the more likely the target audience will pay for what they are promoting.

---

31 Gaille, B. (2013, November 20). How Many Blogs are on the Internet. Retrieved September 8, 2015, from http://www.wpvirtuoso.com/how-many-blogs-are-on-the-internet/

Currently, this is why companies are paying bloggers to promote their products, because they know that bloggers owning trust inside their reader's ideas, thoughts and opinions. *How do I go about actually starting a successful blog?* This is a question you may have asked yourself while reading this chapter. The answer is obvious—you need to start a blog.

START YOUR BLOG

Blogging is free. That's right you read that correctly folks. Free. Choose a website that offers free templates such as WordPress or Blogspot. These sites may not give you the URL that you had your hopes on (a lot of times they are already taken) but you can pay about $10 a year to own that URL that you had your mind set on. When starting a blog, make sure that your brand voice is well developed. You want a blog to reflect your business and brand perfectly.

DEFINE YOUR BRAND

When thinking of what type of blogger you want to be, ask yourself what your interests are. What are your passions and what will you be able to blog about that will not only keep the audience interested- but yourself as well. Be true to who you are as readers will know throughout your writing and design, if it is all for malarkey or show. Be very clear in your thoughts and stay as focused as possible. Do not start a blog just because you want to make a little extra dough in your wallet. Sure, that is a fantastic outcome for having a successful blog but, that shouldn't be your sole purpose. Brands and companies can sense inauthenticity so be honest in your brand and brand voice. Make a list in regards to your personal passions and make this blog a definition of your individuality and uniqueness in this world. There is only one you so no other blog can mimic that if you write for yourself.

DEFINE YOUR TARGET MARKET

If you want frequenters to your blog and through that to build relations with brands and businesses, you need to define who you want your target customer or reader to be. Paint a picture of who you want your target audience to be. What age are they? What are their interests? What trends do they like? How are you similar and different? Be as specific as you can. How can a list of your skills and attributes help this target market? List your achievements and identify who can be helped by your blog. Your expertise should be natural based on your personal brand and blog.

CREATE CONTENT

Now is the time to be creative and create content that is new, fresh, and innovative and truthful to your personal brand or business. Always look back on your goals and objectives and apply that always throughout your content. Envision your target market and keep them in mind whilst writing and creating your content. The best bloggers are the most honest and have their brand voice throughout all of their content. This is the most crucial aspect in order to gain credibility with your target audience and with future businesses and branding. Create the type of content that you would like to read about and that you would consider insightful. Market yourself and your blog as a brand to further engage with potential businesses and brands that you already admire. Ready? Set. Create.

• • •

HASHTAGS HASHED OUT

In life, it is recommended to have a purpose as you go about your day. If you are going to do something, know why you are doing it and then do it well. The principle of hashtagging is no different. Hashtags need to have a purpose also. Hashtagging is part of the implementation to your strategy.

Just to clarify, a hashtag is a word, or multiple words, without any spaces that follows the pound symbol. You can use numbers in the hashtag, but punctuation will break the link of the hashtag and not work properly. Hashtags organize content so social media users can search for the posts, or follow a discussion based on those keywords. For example; the first hashtag, #SanDiegoFire, was created by a Twitter developer in 2007.[32] Twitter handlers searched the hashtag to follow the news of the fire.

32 Hiscott, R. (2013, October 8). The Beginner's Guide to the Hashtag. Retrieved September 29, 2015

Ever since 2007, hashtags have become an integral part of social media, and most major platforms support them. Twitter, Facebook, Instagram, Vine, Pinterest, Tumblr all encourages the use of hashtags.

TWITTER

This was where the hashtag was born. Hashtags on this site are used as a way to organize or follow conversations. When you click on the hashtag there are three ways to sort which posts you see; "Top," "All," "People You Follow." The "Top" options shows the most popular or relevant tweets using the hashtag. "All" shows just that, it includes all of the tweets using the hashtag. "People You Follow" will only include the people you personally follow. These are good options to check in on who is using hashtags or how popular a hashtag has become. You can also search a hashtag, so if you are brainstorming ideas on which one to use, search it to see if it is already in use, and if so how.

VINE

Owned by Twitter, Vine also uses hashtags. In this instance, hashtags are used to maximize shareability. If the hashtags are used to search for vines, you would want to hashtag multiple relevant topics to increase your audience reach.

FACEBOOK

This platform was a little late to the game, and did not add the hashtag until mid 2013.[33] The practice has not been a quick catch. Regardless,

---

33 Hiscott, R. (2013, October 8). The Beginner's Guide to the Hashtag. Retrieved September 29, 2015

the concept is the same, if you click on the hashtag it will take you to a list comprising of posts that use the same hashtag. The results that appear are not limited only to the people you know.

INSTAGRAM

On this platform similarly to others, hashtags are used to organize content. The hashtag typically describes the photo or gives some insight that supplements the photo. Unlike the other platforms Instagram themselves has created hashtags to encourage users to post. One of the most popular is #ThrowbackThursday which urges users to post an old photo on their account with that hashtag. The privacy settings on Instagram come into play during hashtag use. Hashtags only get shared into the public when the profile is not set on private, so for users who want the hashtag to reach a widespread of people, make sure the privacy settings are set accordingly.

TUMBLR

This blogging platform refers to hashtags as a "Tag." The platform has a specific section where you can enter tags and Tumblr automatically adds the hashtag for you. The tags help organize the content by topic, making it easier for users to search for the subject. Only topics entered into the "Tag" section will be linked as a hashtag, items in the main content will not be linked to their searchable database.

PINTEREST

This platform uses hashtags as a primary way to organize content. If users are looking for a specific pin description, they can click the hashtag to explore all the pins with that hashtag. For example if someone was searching for ideas to paint their wall; they could search: wall paint, ideas, color scheme, pinterest would then display any pin with those hashtags used in their description.

A hashtag can be treated as a mini campaign, within your overall social media strategy. You have to go through all the basics that you should be doing for your overall campaign. Ask yourself, or your social media team, what do we want to accomplish? Know what you want to achieve with your hashtag. It could mean gaining followers or creating awareness for a product or an event, but keep that goal in the front of your mind as you use hashtags.

RELEVANCE

Know your audience. At this point, you should be aware of your target audience. Keep them in mind when using hashtags. Browse what they are hashtagging, and join in on the conversation. Whether that is a news story or an entertainment event, your brand needs to be aware of what your customers are interested in, to stay relevant. Hashtagging is not necessarily about hashtagging your brand but adding to the social media conversation. For example; Herschel Supply Co. sells backpacks that people sometimes use to hike with. Instead of hashtagging their brand name they use the hashtag #welltraveled and encourage users to use the hashtag when they post pictures of themselves traveling with the backpack.[34] This is an example of a company knowing their audience well. Herschel Supply Co knows their audience is adventurous and likes to travel. So this hashtag fits the needs of the audience while producing enough buzz to create user generated content. User

---

34 LePage, E. (2014, August 27). How To Use Hashtags: The Do's and Don'ts of hashtags. Retrieved October 3, 2015.

generated content can be very useful for a business. If the quality fits your standards and you have been given the consent of the user, the option available is to re-post it on your own platform.

SHORT & SWEET

When using hashtags, think of the rule Goldilocks; not too big, not too small – just right.[35] Hashtags should be simple and easy to use and understand. To ensure users will include the hashtag in their own content follow the 3 S's; Short, Sweet, and Simple.[36] If the hashtag is too long it will die off quickly and may not even fit in the space given. Think Twitter – users have only 140 characters, make sure your hashtag doesn't take up too many of those. Unless you are using Vine or Pinterest a rule of thumb is 1-3 hashtags at most. You don't want to have more hashtags than words in your post. Or the content is not really your own, but just a bunch of hashtags.

PLAN FOR THE BEST, PREPARE FOR THE WORST

Once you put the content out into the cyber world it is stuck there. Think of all the things that could become of your hashtag, such as your goals and objectives, but also think of the problems that might arise. For example, make sure your hashtag is precise and can be read in one way only, to avoid misinterpretation. Unlike this hashtag: #BlackHateBook.[37] Here there are multiple ways the hashtag could

---

35 Lerner, M. (2014, April 9). 5 Characteristics of a #Successful Hashtag Campaign.
36 Philips, J. (2015, September 26). Hashtag 101: Everything You Need to Know About Creating a Brand Hashtag. Retrieved October 16, 2015.
37 Philips, J. (2015, September 26). Hashtag 101: Everything You Need to Know About Creating a Brand Hashtag. Retrieved October 16, 2015.

be read. It is supposed to read Black Hat eBook; but some could see Black Hate Book, which is not even close to the same, and would surely create a PR nightmare. Or in another instance #McDstories was created with the intention of McDonald's consumers sharing positive stories of their experiences.[38] Instead it turned into people sharing negative experiences and the McDonald's social media team ended up losing control over the hashtag. To avoid these scenarios think of what you can do to prevent them from the beginning.

MAINTAIN/MANAGE

As previously mentioned the hashtag should be treated like a mini campaign. So once the decision is made to create and use a certain hashtag it doesn't stop there. The R2c – repurpose recycle content – model should be taken into consideration here. The hashtag strength should be strong enough that you can reuse it and that your customers can reuse it as well. The length of the hashtag life may vary depending on your goals, but create a hashtag that has the potential to have a long shelf life.

Also noted earlier, by following trends you can use hashtags already gaining traction to interact with your customers. These hashtags put you into the real-time conversation. It is a great way to maintain your presence on social.

There are different ways to manage your hashtag but one is to track and analyze it. Hashtags.org is a great site to follow your hashtag and to monitor how much use it is getting. It offers multiple different services. You can have your hashtag verified, which means making it "official" in a sense. Getting it verified allows you to add your hashtag

---

38 Lerner, M. (2014, April 9). 5 Characteristics of a #Successful Hashtag Campaign.

definition to their dictionary of hashtags. You also can pay for a sub-
scription that permits you to monitor your hashtag while collecting
data and storing it for you.

FAST REFERENCE GUIDE:

- ✓ Consumers looking to bloggers more than ever for credible
  sources
- ✓ Bloggers are now establishing expertise within the advertising
  industry
- ✓ Companies are seeking out bloggers to brand on their per-
  sonal social platforms
- ✓ Companies are now paying bloggers to brand on their social
  platforms
- ✓ Tips on how to start a successful blog
- ✓ Decide what platform works best for your hashtag campaign
- ✓ Make your hashtag relevant
- ✓ Keep your hashtag to the point and easy to read
- ✓ Measure your hashtag campaign

SECTION V Measure

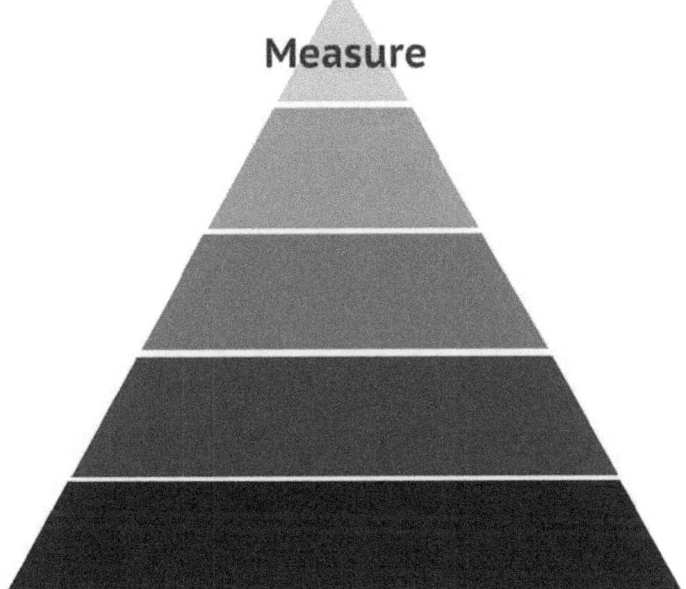

• • •

SOCIAL MEDIA CAMPAIGNS: YOUR GUIDE TO GETTING STARTED

In May of 2014, A1 went through a rebranding initiative transitioning from A1 Steak Sauce to simply A1. They used Facebook to deliver the message to their audience in a simple yet catchy video. The video starts off showing the devoted relationship between "A1 Sauce" and "Steak" that soon is broken by a love affair with "Pork." All of which are personas created on Facebook. Slowly but surely, "A1 Sauce" begins experimenting with other foods and its relationship with "Steak" changes to 'it's complicated' on their Facebook pages. The video wraps up with the understanding that "A1 Sauce" and "Steak" are no longer exclusive but happy with other foods.

You might be thinking, this is a strange way to communicate a rebranding initiative. In its entirety, this social media campaign resulted in 1.4M views, which soaked up 1.6M minutes of YouTube viewing time. That's more than a minute/view on average. To date the video has been liked or shared on Facebook over 6,000 times. [39]This

39 The Best Social Media Campaigns of All Time. (n.d.). Retrieved from https://www.getambassador.com/blog/best-social-media-campaigns

social media campaign was successful in all aspects, now how can you create your own?

WHAT DOES IT MEAN TO CREATE A SOCIAL MEDIA CAMPAIGN?

A social media campaign is a designed and measurable plan intended to convey a message to a targeted audience via social platform. In the past, brands and businesses were encouraged to purely just "join the conversation" on social media. Merely being present on social media is not enough these days to make a difference, a business must be implementing strategic campaigns designed towards their audience.

WHY IS IT CRUCIAL TO DEVELOP A SOCIAL MEDIA CAMPAIGN?

We do not live in a world solely thriving off of print, radio and television ads. Times have changed to a more consumer-based industry. Before social advertising and campaigns, advertising was a one-way street; a marketer would post ads and hope results would follow. Now, when a digital ad or campaign is placed online, results can be tracked by likes, follows, shares, views and more. There are many more opportunities for brands to interact with their audience and actually measure those interactions.

It is crucial to develop a social media campaign so that you have a plan to follow. Set your goals, deadlines, map some content and record where your business currently stands.

HOW DO I START THE PROCESS?

Goals. Plan. Analyze. In that order. I have mentioned goals multiple times to highlight their importance. Don't only just set goals, set objectives. By objectives I mean *specific* goals for your campaign that can be measured afterward, for example: By the end of ___ campaign in 3 months, we want to increase our page likes by 15%.

Plan a process of how you are going to achieve your objective—a strategy. This is the creative part of your campaign process where you decide how you are actually going to reach your objective(s).

Start with an overarching idea that will be broken into a timeline of posts or promotions. For instance, your overarching idea may be that you are going to send out blasts on twitter encouraging user generated content (UGC) to increase interaction. Now you need to take your idea and decide the content required, when, how often and some regulations to your campaign. Before you begin posting to social media, remember to perform several rounds of error checks! Even if an error check consists of personally taking into consideration anything that could possibly go wrong. It is important to organize your plan on a timeline or content calendar to provide an easy way to make sure you are acting on time.

Once you have skillfully implemented your plan, take the necessary time to analyze the results and compare them to your goals. This will be a great opportunity for you to analyze what you did will and what didn't go so well according to the numbers. The flexibility to try and alter campaigns to better fit your audience is the beauty of social media.

Create a social media report and use it gain company buy-in from your colleagues. You may be in a scenario where your company is not inherently a "social brand," meaning social media is not at the forefront of company culture rather it is worked in as an afterthought. Use your positive findings to prove that social media really *does* play a huge role in brand identification and should work hand-in-hand with company initiatives.

As mentioned earlier, it is important to keep in mind that every business has a different company culture thus every social media campaign will be different. Below are 7 tips to help you create a successful social media campaign.

7 TIPS TO CREATING A SUCCESSFUL SOCIAL MEDIA CAMPAIGN

1. **Humanize Your Campaign**
    Whether your goal is to drive engagement through the roof or improve sales for the quarter, connecting with your audience on a personal level is essential. There are many stereotypes associated with large corporations and their level of concern for the "average Joe." To reveal your company as "human" in a professional way will set you apart. An example of this could be as simple as showing warmth to employees or consumers. We are all human; don't be afraid to express it.

2. **Be True to Your Company Voice**
    While developing a comprehensive campaign, it may become easy to lose yourself in the details. At this point in your social efforts, you have already established your brand so stick to it! Your voice is original to *you* and must stay congruent throughout all efforts. It may require you to continuously refer back to what your company's bottom line, or take away message, is and make sure you are still in line.
    If you have not yet established a company "voice," use your branding strategy to help define the direction you will move. For example, an insurance brokerage's voice will be one of expertise and capability whereas an ice cream shop could be one that portrays youth and experimentation.

3. **Actively Engage with Your Audience**
    When you plan your social media campaign, ensure there is room to engage with your audience. This tactic relates

back to humanizing your campaign. Allow the social media platform(s) to act as created: for conversation between communities. You may learn a new identity of your audience or uncover an untapped society by breaking down the barrier between cooperation and consumer. Deter from a one-way campaign, for nothing those include nothing social.

4. **Personalization is Key**

This "tip" is one of the hardest for brands to accomplish. Every company has a different brand, different company culture and different employees. With that being said, only you can determine how to personalize a social media campaign. The most important part is, <u>do not</u> use a cookie cutter campaign. Spend time brainstorming, tweaking and adjusting your plan to make it fit YOUR Company.

5. **Use Trending Hashtags or Topics**

It is nearly impossible to predict what trending topics or hashtags will be next, so how do you work this into your campaign? Know your brand. Know your purpose. Know your buffer zone of what is appropriate to your company voice and use that to your advantage. This is something that should not be exercised until you can answer basic questions about your social media/ brand identity. One of the most successful examples of a brand utilizing a trending topic is during the 2013 Super bowl. The stadium's power surged during the halftime show and immediately Oreo sent a tweet, "Power out? No problem. You can still dunk in the dark." That tweet alone allowed for Oreo to step in front of all other brands that had paid millions for commercials to be run. The key is to stay true to your brand.

6. **Go Where Your Customers Are**

A communications specialist, Bruce Moorehouse, has structured much of his career with 3M around the 40/40/20 rule.

This rule pertains to the amount of weight you should hold on areas of a marketing plan or in this case, a social media campaign. The first 40 percent should be making sure your content is timely, applicable and useful. The second 40 percent should be committed to learning your audience and adjusting your campaign to their needs. The final 20 percent can be dedicated to the creative aspect of the campaign; without worthy content towards the correct audience, creativity does not matter.

When deciding which platform(s) to spread your campaign to, acknowledge your audience and where they might be. For example, if you are a news publication realize that your audience will most likely be on twitter as that is how it is regularly used. If you are more of a visual organization, consider using a visual platform etc. Your worst mistake could be spending a lot of time creating a social media campaign and missing the queue because you did not consider your customer's location.

7. **Clear Calls to Action**

Imagine doing research online for a possible nonprofit to donate your money to, you come across a great campaign highlighting the great work an organization does for homeless children however there is no clear way for you to make a donation. The chances of you moving to the next nonprofit increases with every minute spent searching for a way to donate. Don't let this happen to your customers.

Make clear calls to action (CTA) for your audience to follow to make sure you keep their attention. Even small actions to "learn more here" or "sign up for updates" etc. can help you in the long run. Have someone who has been blind to the creation of the campaign take a test drive and see how they navigate through. You can never assume people will see things the way you see them, so go through tests upon tests.

AFTER IMPLEMENTING YOUR CAMPAIGN, THEN WHAT?

Measure. If something is not measured, it cannot be valued. Make sure your campaign has variables that can be measured to ensure your success. Measure your beginning stats, know where your brand stands and know where you want to go.

Way too often social media campaigns start out by simply distributing content with no real purpose or plan. With each post, measure the rate of success and create a report. You will notice patterns during the week and time of day that are most successful for posting content on each type of platform. Use that to your advantage when creating a social media campaign.

FAST REFERENCE GUIDE:

- ✓ Humanize your campaign
- ✓ Be true to your company voice
- ✓ Actively engage with your audience
- ✓ Personalization is key
- ✓ Use trending hashtags or topics
- ✓ Go where your customers are
- ✓ Clear calls to action
- ✓ Measure

• • •

ABOUT THE AUTHORS

Tatum Major is a Twin Cities native with goals well beyond the land of 10,000 lakes. With a degree in Communications and Journalism and an emphasis in Advertising and Public Relations, she plans on taking her curiosity and passion for the industry out West to pursue a career in Content Management. Her love for people, fiery energy, strength of leadership and vast creative background has helped motivate her career goals greatly.

Contact Tatum:
Email: tatummajor@gmail.com
LinkedIn: http://www.linkedin.com/in/tatummajor

Kaylee Weycker was raised in the city of Kaukauna, Wisconsin and has always dreamed of things far beyond the small town. Pursuing a degree in Communications and Journalism with a General Business minor she strives to work in event planning and marketing. Travel and rescuing animals are two of her biggest passions and she hopes to return to the Kathmandu Valley of Nepal to rescue street dogs.

Contact Kaylee:
Email: kaylee.weycker@gmail.com
LinkedIn: https://www.linkedin.com/in/kaylee-weycker-7a47b491

Emily Sullivan was born and raised in Dubuque, Iowa, surrounded by her parents, Mike & Julie, and three older siblings—Megan, Matt, & Kevin. She now resides in Saint Paul, Minnesota and is pursuing a degree in Communications and Journalism, as well as General Business. As a hardworking woman with a positive attitude, and an outgoing personality, she aspires to work in the professional sports world in public relations, marketing, or social media.

Contact Emily:
Email: sullivan.emily.m@gmail.com
LinkedIn: http://www.linkedin.com/in/emilysullivan6

Paige Gibson was born, raised and currently resides in the Twin Cities. Faith, family and friends have been a priority for Paige since the beginning and those values shape her decisions as she goes about her days. She looks forward with excitement for the next phases of her life. Her ambitious, energetic, and optimistic personality keeps her looking out for the next great opportunity. Paige aspires to be employed in community relations, social media or marketing and may look beyond Minnesota for job opportunities.

Contact Paige:
Email: paigesgibson@gmail.com
LinkedIn: www.linkedin.com/in/paigegibson

Johannah Saari was born in Duluth, Minnesota and studied a Communications and Journalism major in St. Paul. Her curiosity and sense of adventure have lead to dreams of living beyond Minnesota. Her career goals consist of making an impact through her work of communications, marketing or public relations.

Contact Johannah:
Email: Saar6366@gmail.com
LinkedIn: https://www.linkedin.com/in/johannahsaari

Left to Right: Kaylee Weycker, Tatum Major, Johannah Saari, Emily Sullivan, & Paige Gibson
Photo by: Casey Hurley Photography

REFERENCES

Boyer, L. (2014, November 24). Budweiser Ditches Clydesdales to Focus Advertising on Younger Audience. Retrieved October 22, 2015, from http://www.usnews.com/news/articles/2014/11/24/budweiser-ditches-clydesdales-to-focus-advertising-on-younger-audience

Brito, M. (2014). Defining your Brand Story and Content Narrative. In Your brand, the Next Media Company. Que Publishing

Ember, S., & Abrams, R. (2015, September 20). On Instagram and Other Social Media, Redefining 'User Engagement'. Retrieved November 8, 2015.

Ember, S., & Abrams, R. (2015, September 20). On Instagram and Other Social Media, Redefining 'User Engagement'. Retrieved September 8, 2015 http://www.nytimes.com/2015/09/21/business/media/retailers-use-of-their-fans-photos-draws-scrutiny.html?_r=0.

Facebook: Monthly active users 2015 | Statistic. (n.d.). Retrieved October 22, 2015, from http://www.statista.com/statistics/264810/number-of-monthly-active-facebook-users-worldwide/

Fitzgerald, M. (2015, September 8). Social Media Lecture presented at Social Media Ad and PR in University of St. Thomas, Saint Paul.

Fitzgerald, M. (2015, September 29). Social Media Platform Overview [PowerPoint slides].

Gaille, B. (2013, November 20). How Many Blogs are on the Internet. Retrieved September 8, 2015, from http://www.wpvirtuoso.com/how-many-blogs-are-on-the-internet/

Hashtag Analytics for your Brand, Business, Product, Service, Event or Blog. (n.d.). Retrieved October 22, 2015.

Hiscott, R. (2013, October 8). The Beginner's Guide to the Hashtag. Retrieved September 29, 2015.

Hisham, A. (n.d.). How To Choose The Best Social Media For Your Business. Retrieved October 22, 2015, from http://seopressor.com/blog/how-to-choose-social-media-for-business/

How to Repurpose Your Social Media Content [Live Webinar]. (n.d.). Retrieved from http://blog.hubspot.com/marketing/repurpose-content-webinar

Instagram monthly active users 2015 | Statistic. (n.d.). Retrieved October 22, 2015, from http://www.statista.com/statistics/253577/number-of-monthly-active-instagram-users/

Langer, E. (2015, March 20). 140 things you don't know about Twitter. Retrieved October 22, 2015, from http://www.cnbc.com/2014/03/21/140-things-you-dont-know-about-twitter.html

LePage, E. (2014, August 27). How To Use Hashtags: The Do's and Don'ts of hashtags. Retrieved October 3, 2015.

References

Lerner, M. (2014, April 9). 5 Characteristics of a #Successful Hashtag Campaign.

LinkedIn: Numbers of members 2015 | Statistic. (n.d.). Retrieved October 22, 2015, from http://www.statista.com/statistics/274050/quarterly-numbers-of-linkedin-members/

Marshall, C. (2014, September 3). 33 Amazing YouTube Facts and Stats to Tweet and Share. Retrieved October 22, 2015, from http://www.reelseo.com/youtube-facts-stats-2014/

Mosbergen, D. (2015, May 13). You'll Soon Be Able To Order Domino's Pizza On Twitter, Via Pizza Emoji. Retrieved October 22, 2015, from http://www.huffingtonpost.com/2015/05/13/dominos-pizza-emoji-twitter_n_7272138.html

Netflix's View: Internet TV is replacing linear TV. (2015, July 15). Retrieved from http://ir.netflix.com/long-term-view.cfm

Nice Guys Finish First, David Brooks, May 16th 2001, NY Times – Sept. 30th 2015

Philips, J. (2015, September 26). Hashtag 101: Everything You Need to Know About Creating a Brand Hashtag. Retrieved October 16, 2015.

Search engine optimization - Wikipedia, the free encyclopedia. (n.d.). Retrieved November 2, 2015, from https://en.wikipedia.org/wiki/Search_engine_optimization

Smith, C. (2014, August 24). 25 Amazing Vine Statistics. Retrieved October 22, 2015, from http://expandedramblings.com/index.php/vine-statistics/

The 6 Types of Social Media. (n.d.). Retrieved October 22, 2015, from http://seopressor.com/social-media-marketing/types-of-social-media/

The Best Social Media Campaigns of All Time. (n.d.). Retrieved from https://www.getambassador.com/blog/best-social-media-campaigns

The History of Social Media and its Impact on Business - Simeon Edosomwan, Minot State University Sitalaskshmi Kalangot Prakasan, Minot State University Doriane Kouame, Minot State University Jonelle Watson, Minot State University, Tom Seymour, Minot State University, used Sept. 30th 2015

What Is Evergreen Content? Beginner's Guide to Evergreen Content | WordStream. (n.d.). Retrieved from http://www.wordstream.com/blog/ws/2012/10/16/guide-to-evergreen-content-marketing

Writing S.M.A.R.T. Goals. (n.d.). Retrieved October 22, 2015, from http://www.hr.virginia.edu/uploads/documents/media/Writing_SMART_Goals.pdf